Maxim Murashka

One Flew Over the Cuckoo's Nest - 2 or reputation

Maxim Murashka

One Flew Over the Cuckoo's Nest - 2 or reputation

On real events

Drugoe Reshenie

Imprint
Any brand names and product names mentioned in this book are subject to trademark, brand or patent protection and are trademarks or registered trademarks of their respective holders. The use of brand names, product names, common names, trade names, product descriptions etc. even without a particular marking in this work is in no way to be construed to mean that such names may be regarded as unrestricted in respect of trademark and brand protection legislation and could thus be used by anyone.

Cover image: www.ingimage.com

Publisher:
Drugoe Reshenie
is a trademark of
International Book Market Service Ltd., member of OmniScriptum Publishing Group
17 Meldrum Street, Beau Bassin 71504, Mauritius

Printed at: see last page
ISBN: 978-613-8-38435-9

In pursuit of profit, FG Brokercreditservice's "great mind" personified by Mr. Vitaly Shelikhovsky met with another "great mind" - a provincial shares buyer named Maxim Murashka. Their encounter brings forth a barrage of conclusions. Based on a true story. Reportage. NUMBERS are a must, otherwise it's impossible to understand the stock market..

CHAPTER 1. THE PURCHASE

EPISODE 1 NATURE. MORNING. IN THE STREETS OF NOVOSIBIRSK

JANUARY 2001

Short interdictions / along with titles and music / fragments (3-5 seconds each):
The streets of Novosibirsk; Max and Vasiliev are walking.(they will always be dressed in a standard way. Max: jeans, T-shirt, good shoes, stylish jacket or sweatshirt, a beanie hat; Volodya: (formal outfit) business suit, business-style shoes, a long jacket, a formal-style hat.)

EPISODE 2 INTERIOR, ENTRY HALL AT BCS. DAYTIME

/Titles, the music is still playing/

THE INTERVIEW

Max and Vasilyev enter the hall of the BCS office (the name and type of company can be seen from the sign at the entrance and the logo in the hall).
Max glances at his watch - it's 12.55. He approaches the semicircular table where the secretary sits. He nods and says something to Max. Walking away from the table, Max nods to Vasilyev in the direction of the couch against the wall.
Both walk over to it and sit down.
Employees pass through the hall, from office to office (with still, indifferent faces)
Vasilyev turns his head to Max a couple of times, as if wanting to say something, but then changes his mind.

MAX

We come by a recommendation, so everything should go smoothly. I suggest we agree between ourselves - on the interest.

VASILyEV

(nods)What do you say?

MAX

As we usually do, 50 x 50... With all financial matters left to ME!

VASILyEV
(with obvious relief)
Yes, of course.

A tall, energetic employee comes into the hall

SHELIKHOVSKY
(throws a tenacious glance at the partners and extends his hand to Max)
Glad to meet you! Vitaly Shelikhovsky!

MAX
(shaking the hand)
Maxim Murashka

VASILIEV
(shaking the hand) Vasilyev... Vladimir

SHELIKHOVSKY
Follow me.

EPISODE 3 INT. SHELIKHOVSKY'S OFFICE. DAY.

A small bright room. Shelikhovsky, with Max and Vasilyev to his right, with Max closer, sit at a T-shaped negotiations table.

SHELIKHOVSKY
Let's get to business...
(his tone changes from slightly relaxed to dry and hard)
Where have you worked before?

MAX
I'm on the market since 1997. Here.... and here.... and also here... (Including BKF Horizon LLC, with unclear relevance to the plot: that company's CEO had been murdered).

On hearing the answer, Shelikhovsky tilts his head a bit to the side, somewhat surprised.

SHELIKHOVSKY
Why did you stop cooperation at all those places?

MAX

Due to crises.

Shelikhovsky turns his head toward Vasilyev.

VASILYEV
An the securities department, at Kuzbassenergo.

SHELIKHOVSKY
(nodding)
What do you know about BCS?

MAX
(growing enthusiastic)
The company is among the top three at the stock market... Like "Troika Dialog".

SHELIKHOVSKY
(looks up from the table at Max)
I say we are better than Troika Dialog!

Max shrugs - he obviously doesn't care.

SHELIKHOVSKY
So (he puts both his palms on the table... What are you planning to do now? (As if he doesn't know).

MAX
We're ready to accept papers from the population. The office is ready and promoted, with our people sitting in the registers...

VASILYEV
At Kuzbassenergo, everyone knows me.

SHELIKHOVSKY
What can we do for you?

MAX
Money...

SHELIKHOVSKY
Money ... (throws a tenacious glance first at Max, then looks over to Vasilyev).

MAX
Yeah, you give us money - and leave us alone.

Shelikhovsky again takes a quick look at Max, and smirks. Pause.

SHELIKHOVSKY

How much do you want?

MAX

About two hundred thousand...

Pause (lasts a second, two, three...)

SHELIKHOVSKY

(looking slightly aside)
What's my reward?

MAX

30% of net profit.

Now Max is looking at the reaction of the person sitting in front of him - but there is none.

Shelikhovsky takes his office phone and dials a number.

SHELIKHOVSKY

Bykov, I need you at my office.

EPISODE 3 INT. SHELIKHOVSKY'S OFFICE. DAY.

BYKOV. THE BEGINNING

A cheerful and extremely handsome (the fashion-model type) Bykov enters the office. He and Shelikhovsky exchange glances. Vasilyev follows Bykov as he walks from one to the other partner. Max is still staring in front of himself.

BYKOV

Will you help bring "Azot" to the stock exchange? Shares are in the register.

Bykov sits down to the table in front of the two partners, and puts a folder in front of himself.

MAX

You're interested in "Azot"?

BYKOV

Yes.

Max looks at Shelikhovsky.

MAX

(stressing every syllable, meaningfully)

We will take a lot of these papers!

Bykov opens the folder in front of him and lays the documents out on the table. Then, smiling, he looks at Max.

BYKOV

I've got three documents here: with price and without quantity, with quantity and without price, with price and quantity.

Bykov looks at Max, anticipating questions (like, why three?).

Max rakes the documents from the table, saying nothing.

MAX

How much does Kuzbassenergo cost today?

BYKOV

7 cents.

MAX

What a shame... To fall from a dollar to seven cents...

Bykov smiles, spreading his hands.

SHELIKHOVSKY

Go to the back office, they'll take your passport copies... I'll call you on Friday.

Shelikhovsky rises, making it clear that the meeting is over.

The partners also rise and leave.

EPISODE 5 INT. BCS OFFICE. DAY

Max and Vasilyev are at the exit from the BCS office.

VASILYEV
He never said anything about the interest.

MAX
Apparently, we'll decide that as we go, like we always do.

EPISODE 6
Documentary footage from 2001: TV news/ newspaper pages (stock exchange). Marquee: we buy securities...

EPISODE 7 INT. APARTMENT OF MAX'S PARENTS. LATE MORNING.

IRINA

Morning. Opening his eyes, and lying on his side, Max sees in front of him a bedside table with a night lamp, and a watch next to it. He slowly sits up. At this moment, he notices a sleeping girl beside him. He shuts his eyes tight, then opens. Looks at the girl. Shrugs, gets out of bed.

Turning around, Max sees that the girl has already opened her eyes and is looking at him.

MAX

Let me introduce myself... Murashka Maxim

IRINA
(smiling)
Irina Bezdenezhnykh

MAX
(smiling)
Our mutual friend Vasya has told me about you.

IRINA
(lazily sitting up in bed)
And what did you say?

MAX
(smiling)
Said you were silly.

IRINA
Did he say so?

MAX
Yep, he said so. (looks at Irina, but the faint grimace on her face doesn't send a clear message of how she took his words). How is it going with his double romance? With Veronika, and with Julia - your sister...

IRINA
One day he's with Veronica - (spreads his hands), and the other - with Julia. What a scoundrel.

MAX
(nods)
We tried seducing one girl together... once... And it worked. (grins) But they sent me off, to take a walk...

IRINA
(smiles) I know. He told everyone about this.

MAX
What a scoundrel. Alright. I am going back to work after a six-month vacation. Will be buying shares from the population. (abruptly gets out of bed) I need to make a call.

IRINA
Congratulations! (looking at Max as he gets out of bed) And I am writing my graduation paper.

EPISODE 8. MAX's PARENTS' APARTMENT. LATE MORNING.

Max is on the phone.

MAX
...Yes, with Shelikhovsky, and with Bykov.... I've talked to them three times already! Everything is falling together. We'll be starting to buy. Keeping in touch through Bykov. We'll have the money tomorrow. Documents in your name will come with a bus. Two positions. Purchase price approved. Kuzbassenergo -1.7, Azot - 22.
Get two TV channels to advertise us, just one day - on Sunday. While we are alone in the market, let them think we don't need that many securities.

VASILYEV
What must I announce?

MAX
Kuzbassenergo - 1.5, Azot - 18.

VASILIEV
Clear.

MAX
How much money do you have?

VASILYEV
Two hundred thousand.

MAX
And I have something around that sum as well. Very decent for a start.

Max looks out the window - sunny weather, clouds running across the sky.

transition to episode 9.

EPISODE 9. NAT. STREET NEAR MAX'S OFFICE. MORNING

BIG CLIENT

Clouds running across the sky. City streets, honking cars. Max walks up to the office building. The building is old and shabby. The same unattractive view of the corridors he walks along.

Max opens the door and goes into the office. In the office sits one person - Vasilyev. He's at a desk, talking on the phone. A clock on the wall shows 10.00.

Max takes out a bundle of bills from his briefcase, puts them on the table in front of Vasilyev. Vasilyev hangs up.

MAX
Fifty gran. From BCS's friends. On receipt (clarifies in response to Vasilyev's questioning glance) Some coal dealers.

VASILYEV
We're about to have a visit from shareholders....

His phone rings again.

MAX
(into the phone)
Hellooooo

FEMALE VOICE
Do you buy "Azot" shares?

MAX
Yes, we buy them... still...

FEMALE VOICE
For how much?

MAX
18 rubles

FEMALE VOICE
Will you give more?

MAX
No

FEMALE VOICE (after a short pause)
What's your address?

MAX
Kuznetsky Prospect, 41-37

EPISODE 10 INT. MAX'S OFFICE/BCS OFFICE
Clock on the wall shows 13.00

The phone rings. Max picks up.

BYKOV
Hi Maxim.

MAX
Hey

BYKOV
The bus will arrive at 13.00, take the documents from the driver.

MAX
I'm out of money.

BYKOV
How's that?

MAX
We bought shares...

BYKOV
What kind of? For how much?

MAX
A thousand of Azot's, 22 apiece, Kuzbassenergo 12,000, for 1.7. As we have discussed.

BYKOV
(smiling)
Your job is to buy cheaper, and my job is to sell for more.

Max is silent.

BYKOV
And how did you buy without documents?

MAX
With blank forms... Don't you know that when a shareholder sees money, he doesn't care what to sign...

BYKOV
That's American style... May I... (after a short pause) Okay. In the evening I'll call you again; I'll settle this, with the money.

Max hangs up.

MAX
(Vasilyev, looking at the documents that have just arrived) In whose name are we buying?

VASILYEV
Cyprus LTD. Beneficiaries: Director, Vitaly Shelikhovsky...

MAX
So, Shelikhovsky is apparently a cool dude - look, a beneficiary!

VASILYEV
Yeah.

EPISODE 11 INT. MAX'S OFFICE. DAY

Max enters the office, puts a pack of bills on the table in front of Vasilyev. They exchange gazes.

MAX
150,000 rubles from friends, but without a receipt this time.

VASILYEV
Should be enough for a day or two. I took to the register all that we bought yesterday...

MAX
(making notes in the cash book)
Income, 150,000 rubles, 6000 on top, you can have your half.

Max looks up, and sees a smiling Vasilyev.

The phone rings.

BYKOV
Hi, how are you?

MAX
Got 150,000, shareholders are coming in; while we are alone on the market, we buy, as agreed, Kuzbassenergo at 1.7 per share, and Azot, at 22.

BYKOV
So ... (acts surprised) But I don't have these shares!

MAX
How come you don't?

BYKOV
I don't see them in the account.

MAX
The papers are on the way... The ones from yesterday are already in the register...

BYKOV
And ones from today?

MAX
The ones from today are in the desk. Do we have to go to the register every day?

BYKOV
I go to the register twice a day (for this he needs to simply walk to the other side of his office building).

MAX
(after a short pause) Bye! I will call you when I have news...

EPISODE 12

News chronicle - MICEX, then immediately work at the BCS office.

SWITCH to the BCS office in episode 13

EPISODE 13 INT. BCS OFFICE/ MAX'S OFFICE. DAY

At Bykov's desk in the trading room stands one of the employees, showing him some documents. Bykov's phone rings. He pick up.

BYKOV
(with a smile)
Hello!

MAX
A big customer. 30,000 of "Azot."

BYKOV
(with a mix of surprise and distrust in his tone)
30,000!?

MAX
Yes. The client is sitting in the hallway. I haven't named the price. Talk to him yourself...

BYKOV
Give him to me.

Bykov shovels documents from his desk, gives them to the employee and makes an impatient gesture - "we're finished." The employee moves away from the desk.

Max stands up from the table, opens the door to the hall. A well-dressed young man stands at the window at the end of the corridor, and, hearing the sound of the opening door, turns to Max.

MAX
Come on in... They'll talk to you.

The man enters the office, takes the phone that Max gives him.

CUSTOMER
How much can you offer?

BYKOV
32 rubles per share.

CUSTOMER
How are we going to make a deal? I am interested in cash.

BYKOV
Tomorrow in the registry at noon. I will come myself.

switch to Max and Vasilyev alone in the office.

MAX
Wow (to Bykov)
960 thousand rubles! (smiles).

BYKOV
So who is he? (his tone betrays his tension)

MAX
I don't know. He left his phone number with us, said he knows the registrar.

BYKOV
I'll come tomorrow afternoon with security. You will go to the registry with me.

MAX
Throw in some money for work.

BYKOV

I will.

EPISODE 14 INT. REGISTER OF AZOT SHAREHOLDERS. MORNING.

By frame, abruptly: All participants of the transaction drive up to the registrar's office. Bykov arrives in a jeep; the partners get out of a taxi.

They enter the registrar's office.

The last ones are Max and the guard.

A large shabby room.

Max looks at the security guard with curiosity: "He's a mountain!" The client is already in the office with his partner. They all greet each other.

BYKOV
My condition is, I pay only after I am notified that the shares have come to my account.

REGISTRAR
Of course, I can speed up the process, but I know this man (nods at the client)... There will be no problem.

BYKOV
Doesn't matter. Notification first.

MAX(looking at the bars on the windows) **"And nowhere to run."**

BYKOV
(whispers)
Shut up.

CLIENT
(glancing at Bykov who's intensely awaiting response)
Agreed. (shrugs slightly).

EPISODE 15 NAT. STREET NEAR THE AZOT SHAREHOLDERS REGISTER. DAY.

The parties of the transaction go out on the street.
The client leaves.
Bykov gets in the car with his security. The partners stand on the sidewalk.

MAX
Alexey, so who bought this package?

BYKOV
(with an expression on his face that says: I have everything falling together here so smoothly, and now you come with this very unnecessary question)
I cannot answer this question at the moment.

Bykov's car leaves. Max watches it till it's out of sight, and then turns to Vasilyev.

MAX
They - (nods at the building they just left) - also bought two really decent packages of shares, in a week... 5,000, Azot shares, and 100,000 Kuzbassenergo shares - at a good price. Life has become easier... Life has become more fun.

Max and Vasilyev head towards the bus stop.

EPISODE 16 INT. HOSTEL. LATE EVENING.
"LIFE HAS BECOME MORE FUN"

A hostel room. A minimum of furniture. No wallpaper. The whole group is sitting on the floor in front of a TV. Everyone's spirits are high.

VASILY
So we're all here, what shall we do?

MAX
What options do we have? Smoke a joint. Get to it, you're the man!

Vasily gets up, and starts getting the weed ready.

JULIA
I have a tape with Beavis and Butthead cartoons...

IRINA

Aha, that's cool. (laughs)

Julia inserts the tape into the video player.

MAX
(breathing out smoke) What are these cartoons?

IRINA
What, you've not seen these before? That's an MTV hit!

They all take turns smoking the joint.

VASILY
It's about two morons who are forever watching the TV. Wait until it comes… (meaning the effect from smoking weed)

JULIA
I already feel it!

IRINA
Me too...

MAX
(exchanges glances with Vasily, shrugs) Vasya and I are tough(laughs).

VASILY
(laughs)
Now we got it.

They watch the cartoons.

VASILY
I am Butthead, and you are Beavis!

MAX
No, I am Butthead, and you are Beavis! Ladies, judge us!

JULIA
One thing I can say for sure - we have two idiots on the screen, and two idiots here in this room!

IRINA

Butthead is the leader, so Butthead is Max

MAX (TO VASILY)
You have never been to Harlem! You will never be in Harlem! You'll be here all your life, sitting on your ass! You are stupid! You have no money and no one will ever give you any!!!

VASILY
Shut up, freak! Your mom is a whore.

Vasily looks at Julia, but she pretends that what is happening doesn't concern her.

MAX
(noticing Vasily's reaction)
Alright, party's over... Irina, let us go to furnished rooms!

VASILY
Y-yeah... Fuck, fuck and fuck more!

EPISODE 17 INT. MAX'S OFFICE. DAY.

Short interruptions - 2-3 seconds.
Max's office, purchase of shares:
Different clients - different emotions - some aren't hiding their joy and are beaming; others are tense and suspicious...

A MIDDLE AGED MAN
(in a disappointed tone) I thought it would be much more... Enough to buy a car, a flat...

VASILYEV
Yesterday you had nothing. Tomorrow, you may have nothing again. Sell while someone still needs these pieces of paper.

ELDERLY WOMAN
I could never have dreamed to be selling shares one day! And it all happened at once, and now, here I am... I thought we were just given these papers, but everything will be the same old way...

VASILYEV
And perhaps it will be the same old way, - but another time. And now...

He puts a bundle of bills in front of her...

EPISODE 18 INT. MAX'S OFFICE. MORNING.

COMPETITORS

Brief interruptions:
Another client signs the document - VasilYev submits documents to the registER - Bykov sees the receipt of shares

On the phone with Bykov.

BYKOV
I have some interesting information for you.

MAX
What is it?

BYKOV
The people you take money from will also buy stocks ...

Pause

MAX
That's all, we will take nothing else. Prices are going up.
(annoyed)

BYKOV
You will have the same price with them, according to the contract, Azot 22, Kuzbassenergo 1.7.

Pause

MAX
I agree on 22 for Azot. But, for Kubassenegro… between us... and your friends... some tough competition is at hand!

EPISODE 19 NAT. CITY STREET. DAY.

Max and Vasilyev are having lunch in a cafe that has very few modestly dressed visitors.

VASILYEV
And why does BCS need this? Shareholders have told me already. We won't be able to work.

MAX

Raise the prices... Azot, 22, Kuzbassenego, -1.7-2.1, advertise on all channels, for the whole week, learn everything about them, make calls.

Switch to:
Late evening. Max is at home. The phone rings - he picks up.

VASILYEV
I found out... they are somewhere on the outskirts, all cool and stuff, coal miners, you see...

MAX
Amateurs - I see... Goodbye, Azot's surplus...

EPISODE 20 INT. MAX'S OFFICE. MORNING, DAY, EVENING
Work with shareholders: Money-paper.
Azot shareholders:
Different types, age.
Elderly partners are shown where to sign; older people see poorly, they squint; they are very happy to be getting the money. Their clothes are poor.

Kuzbassenergo shareholders are better dressed.
Max writes a report.

EPISODE 21 INT. BCS OFFICE. NOVOSIBIRSK. DAY.

A VISIT TO BCS

Cut-ins:
Max's arrival in Novosibirsk. On the way to the office, he glances at the same details as on his first visit with Vasilyev - something has changed, something has remained the same.

Max reaches the BCS office. Walks down the hall with Bykov. Shelikhovsky comes out of his office.

SHELIKHOVSKY
Greetings! So, how do you like us? (mockingly)

MAX
Fine.

Smiling, Bykov nods, as if in confirmation of Max's words.

BYKOV
Follow me, please.

EPISODE 22 INT. TRADERS AREA AT BCS. DAY.

In the main hall - trading.

BYKOV

(pointing to the screen) Watch me sell.

Sells.

The trading system shows trades in Yukos stocks, once they are bought, the price escalates.

Bykov is confused - he wanted to show how expensive it is. Max is unruffled.

MAX

You sold cheaply.

BYKOV

(In a professional manner)

Calculate the financial result. So far it's only Kuzbassenergo.

MAX

Good. We will not even touch Azot. (speaks in a hard tone)

EPISODE 23 INT. BCS TRADER. DAY.

Sitting next to Murashka, Bykov finishes his calculations, unfolds the sheet and pushes it towards Max.

BYKOV

...32,000, sign here.

Max signs. Thinks for a moment. Then turns to the employee sitting at a computer.

MAX

Show me the Kuzbassenergo selling price.

The employee opens the terminal. He hits one key, and Bykov, who wanted to stop him, does not have the time to do so. The screen shows 2.5 rubles.

MAX

(to Bykov)

2.5

BYKOV

(to the employee, with a smile, after a short pause - the employee clearly doesn’t understand that he has done something wrong) Why did you show?

Max looks at Bykov, but Bykov gets up from the table and leaves the office.

Switch to: Bykov enters Shelikhovsky's office.
Vitaly is sitting at the table, listening to the speakerphone conversation of Max and his staff - it becomes clear that he is listening to everyone.

Switch to Bykov, who returns and puts the paper with calculations on the desk. The paper is signed by Shelikhovsky; 20%.

Max shakes his head and crosses his signature.

MAX

Thirty percent

An awkward silence follows.

MAX

(points to numbers, strongly)

And here is a mistake!
According to my calculations, excluding Azot - 50,000. 38,000, ok?

Pause

BYKOV

Okay... go to the cashier.

EPISODE 24 BCS OFFICE. DAY.

2-3 second cut-ins:
Bills "flipping" in the money counting machine. Max takes bills, puts them in bundles, stuffs them into his "shahid belt." (T-shirt with a curved edge, on a rope, with brick-shaped secret pockets).

From the shot of him with bills in hand move to Episode 25

EPISODE 25 INT. MAX'S OFFICE. DAY.

MAX
I received an advance of 38,000, the question of open interest is... (showing the paper)

Pause. Vasilyev is silent.

MAX
Volodya, do you remember how on our second day of work I caught you "red-handed"?

Vasilyev looks at Max, meets his eyes

Max goes on:
When I just stepped out of the office...

VASILYEV
(looks away) I remember.

MAX
I impose a 10,000 fine on you - it's my exclusive right.

VASILYEV
(After a quick nod, says as he looks at the table)
Yes of course.

EPISODE 26 INT. MAX'S OFFICE. DAY. FINANTIAL ALLIANCE. RALLY. A COLLECTIVE PACKAGE.

Short cut-ins (switching):
Money-papers, money-papers.
Work, buying shares: shareholders of different kinds (age, manner of behaving during the sale and purchase process, etc).

Max picks up the phone, calls Bykov.

MAX
(laughs) Alexey, and now - guess what, I have some interesting information for you...

BYKOV
What is it?

MAX
A certain "Financial Alliance" popped up on the market, and it seems like a matter of honor for them - 2 rubles more than a shareholder gives us...

BYKOV
And what's so funny?

MAX
The agreement with our friends no longer makes sense. We have a market economy now.

BYKOV
I see.

Max hangs up, but the phone rings again.

SHELIKHOVSKY
You? You took five?... Five?..

MAX
(surprised) 5 percent?

SHELIKHOVSKY
Why?

MAX
Friends...

Pause.

SHELIKHOVSKY
Maybe you should think about changing your job...

MAX
(grinning)
Same old, same old...

Max hangs up.

EPISODE 27 INT. MAX'S OFFICE/ ALLIANCE'S OFFICE. DAY.

Silence (2-3 seconds):

Max - 24, Alliance -26, Max - 28, Alliance -30, Max -32.
One office, then another office (competitor's)
The door closes behind the next client.
The clock's hour hand marks another hour - and no one comes; another hour - still no clients...

VASILYEV
The shareholders have grown quiet, they barely come…

MAX
That's clear - once the rally has begun, they wait until prices go up...

ALLIANCE
(into the handset) - 32

MAX
We'll keep on like this.

VASILYEV
A certain Valentina Sergeyevna called from Azot, said that they had collected a package of 50,000 shares at the company. She wants to meet...

MAX
A collective package. Call her, let her come

EPISODE 28 INT. MAX'S OFFICE/ BCS OFFICE. DAY.

Max and Vasilyev meet Valentina Sergeyevna in the office.
They sit at the table. A short pause.

VALENTINA SERGEEVNA
We chose you.

MAX
You made the right choice.

VALENTINA SERGEEVNA
(puts papers on the table)
Here are the lists, 50,000 pieces, I'm interested in... First of all, the price...

VASILYEV
And second of all?

VALENTNA SERGEEVNA
And secondly - what will I have from this?

MAX
Just a minute

Max picks up the phone and calls Bykov

MAX
Alexey, 50,000 from Azot, from a certain Valentina Sergeyevna, talk to her...

BYKOV
Alright!

BYKOV
Here's my offer: 52, and a ruble from each stock goes to you, but it must be done quickly.

VALENTINA SERGEEVNA
Agreed. Tomorrow morning people will start coming in.

BYKOV
Very well. We will be there tomorrow morning.

Quick flashes: Max and Bykov look at their watches and the clock on the wall, in turn, at different times, and in different locations, subconsciously expecting a serious event/a big transaction. They want to rush time. It gets dark, and then, the morning comes.

EPISODE 29 INT. MAX'S OFFICE. MORNING.

SHILOV
Morning. Stacks of passports on the table.

Bykov enters the office with a suitcase, a security guard, and a young, handsome man of about 20 (he is the employee from the trading area who showed Max the Kuzbassenergo price).

BYKOV
Here, meet Slava Shilov, he will help us.

MAX
Why didn't Shelikhovsky come? (sarcastically)

SLAVA
He was going to... (smiling)

Bykov, Shilov and the partners sit down to do paperwork.

Every once in a while, shareholders come into the office.

The phone never stops ringing.

Max stops filling our papers (as it's not his duty anyway).

Interlock: Max gets up from the table and walks around the office, looking at those sitting at the table.
Drinking tea... smoking... drinking tea...

Negotiating with shareholders.

MAX
That's interesting, but what do we announce now?

Bykov looks up from the papers, at Max.

Max continues:
I propose the following: reduce the price, as if we no longer need the shares... (In response to Bykov and Vasilyev's surprised look). What are we losing anyway?..

BYKOV
I agree.

Max abruptly gets up from the table, looks out into the corridor. There is a big queue

MAX
And how will we buy?

BYKOV
I go first (opens the suitcase with the money).

EPISODE 30 INT. MAX'S OFFICE. DAY

Bykov buys shares (1-2 seconds cut-ins) money-papers, money-papers.

BYKOV
(watching the next shareholder) Uh... Bought.

BYKOV
(to Max) Valentina Sergeyevna could have gotten less... a thousand to twenty... (looks at Max expectantly)

MAX
No. Pay it off yourself.

Bykov sums his work up:

BYKOV
It all fits, and there's 20 rubles left (grins). Now you buy (puts the remaining money on the table)

Murashka: paper money

The door closes after the next client

MAX

Bought.

Looks at the documents.

MAX

It all fits, and there are 500 rubles left.

Pause.

BYKOV

(making a weak gesture with his hand)

Oh, come on!

MAX

(puts the money into his wallet)

According to the law of the box office - all that's on top is mine. And all that is below the tip, is mine as well...

The guard (Zolotov) pretends to be reaching for his gun.

The phone rings, Max picks up.

SHELIKHOVSKY

How is the process going?

MAX

Fine.

SHELIKHOVSKY

How much money do you need for tomorrow?

MAX

About two million.

SHELIKHOVSKY

They will bring it in the afternoon, keep it here for now.

EPISODE 31 INT. MAX'S OFFICE. DAY.

Bykov finishes writing the reports and prepares to leave the office with his security guy. He is almost walking out, holding the handle of the open door when Max addresses him.

MAX
Alexey - wait! Tell me, how much did you buy?

Pause.

BYKOV
I bought 18,000.

MAX
(picks up the book)
Okay, then we'll write this down: Bykov bought 18,000 shares.

Bykov stares at Max for a moment, and then leaves the office.

EPISODE 32 INT. MAX'S OFFICE. EVENING.

Max is standing by the window with a cup of tea in his hand. Slava sits in a chair. Vasilyev fills out the documents.

MAX
Money spent, papers sorted. Slava, you will sleep at Volodya's. Tomorrow is a big day.

Max turns from the window to Vasilyev

MAX
(to Vasilyev)
Bykov cheated Valentina Sergeevna for 20,000. Why does he care? He won't have to work with her anymore.

Max grins wryly, meets gazes with
Slava and leaves the office.

VASILYEV
Let's go home.

Stuffs all the papers into his
bag.

EPISODE 33 INT. MAX'S OFFICE. MORNING.

More and more new shareholders walk towards the office.

There are dozens of passports on the table in the office, Vasilyev is working non-stop.

VASILYEV
(Filling the
documents)

MAX
Who can go buy some cigarettes?

Slava raises his head.

SLAVA
I'll go.

The door closes behind Slava.

MAX
(glances at the door) Who is
this Slava?

VASILYEV
Shelikhovsky's cousin. Recently
returned from the army. He served
in the Navy, and then his
relatives sent him to
Novosibirsk. Says there are way
too many traders out there…

MAX
Got you.

Slava returns.

MAX

Slava, this is for you (pushes a pile of papers towards him) - you will fill them.

Shilov's mobile phone rings.

SLAVA
(To Shelikhovsky) I will leave in the evening - I see no point in being here.

The hour hand of the clock on the wall makes two turns.

The phone rings, and Max picks up.

SHELIKHOVSKY
How many are you planning to buy today?

MAX
37,000. We submit papers to the register when we can.

SHELIKHOVSKY
The car will come after lunch, you will get 2, and send your report with Shilov.

EPISODE 34 INT MAX'S OFFICE. EVENING

Max is writing a report.

VASILYEV
The shareholders have heard rumors of some kind of package, that's all. Prices went down. The Alliance has stopped giving money...

Max distracts from his papers. Pause.

MAX

The Alliance has run out of money… It will take them time to buy, start, sell, and get the money... And we have money for BCS! So, they started **panicking!** Slava, we need another jeep for Monday. We will buy a lot of shares!

CHAPTER 2. TRAGIC ACCIDENT

EPISODE 35 NATURE IN THE STREET OF THE CITY. DAY.

TRAGIC ACCIDENT

Max, Irina and Julia are walking down the street.

MAX

Vasya is doing repairs somewhere. We are having rest. I suggest that we go to a nice place... To drink and have a quick bite.

GIRLS

(almost in unison)

We agree.

EPISODE 36 INT. CAFE/RESTAURANT. EVENING

Semi-empty hall of an inexpensive cafe. Music is playing.

MAX

...Of course, both of you (he points in turns at the girls) are the type of women Vasya and I can characterize as ours.
You are educated, cynical, you have low self-esteem, no matter what to do with you or what to say to you. And ... what is important - you are nympho ...

JULIA

Thanks for your compliment.

MAX

And relatively indifferent to money.

IRINA

I have never had it... And I am not sure I will ever have... My surname is Bezdenezhnykh which is 'Nomoney'. But maybe it is all ahead of me.

JULIA

No point depending on things. It is important to become a complete person without it. Then it will probably appear. Maybe ... For now, the main thing is that my chief accountant’s salary is enough to live on.

MAX

Enough about money. Another 100 grams.

Max is pouring alcohol into glasses.

MAX

Yulia, Vasya told me what you were up to when you floated down the river. I promise - I will never tell anyone.

JULIA

Hope so.

MAX

Irina, are you able to do the same?

IRINA

What?

MAX

I won't tell you. Julia, what to you think about Vasya's parallel romance with Veronika?

JULIA
(sighing and pausing between words) This is a difficult question. And I even help him ...

MAX
Another 100.

They clink glasses and drink.

MAX
You know my propensity to fall into abstraction. But if everything could be rewound back, then it would have been better for us, Vasya and I, to switch places ...

IRINA
Why so?

MAX
Irina you have a domineering nature. Control is important to you, over a man. I'll break you. Potential conflict. (leans back in his chair, looks at Julia) And Julia doesn't care on which side is the power. It's easier with her.

JULIA
Oh, thanks for a compliment... (Julia nods her head, flirting).

IRINA
(looking down at the table) To switch places...

Irina gets up abruptly and goes away.

MAX
What a quirk? Objection! (After her)

JULIA
We are competitors. (smiling insicively)

Max watches Irina's back, takes the bottle and pours it again in glasses.

MAX
Another 100. Let's go to my place

JULIA
(after a short pause - without turning her head, she throws a short glance in the direction of the departed Irina) Let's go.

EPISODE 37 NATURE. IN THE STREET CLOSE TO THE MAX'S HOUSE. NIGHT

Max and Julia are standing at the open door of the taxi next to them.

JULIA
So what now?

MAX
(pausing between words) I ... for now ... keep quiet.

JULIA
Considering that we live in one room - it is difficult to hide and keep silent. And I do not want that. And Vasya ... (she looks askance at Max)

MAX
And what about Vasya? Feel like a scoundrel? No.(shakes his head shortly), it was payback for him.

EPISODE 38 NATURE. IN THE STREET. DAY

Irina is walking down the street. Slows down a step, stops, thinking about something. Turns around - goes back, but takes only a few steps and, once again, turns, goes further ... Turning at the corner of the house, she sees Max standing by the cafe. Slowly walks over to him.
Stops nearby.

MAX
You know?

IRINA
I know.

MAX
Do you need me strongly?

IRINA
Strongly.

MAX
I understand ... You can follow me as much as you like. Someday you will understand what love is. Let's go to my place. I still need to talk with Vasya.

IRINA
Let's go.

EPISODE 39 INT. MAX'S PARENTS FLAT. DAY.

Without taking off his clothes, Max answers the phone and dials the number.

VASILY
Yes...Talk to me...

MAX
Probably, it's you who needs to talk.

VASILY
Oh, really?... I am still at work...

MAX
I have nothing to say in my defense. Why are you so excited? (smirking)

VASILY
It's not what you think.

MAX
How do you know what I think.
What can I remind to you?

VASILY
I don't want to continue the
conversation any longer.

MAX
Ok, bye.

EPISODE 40 INT. MAX'S FLAT. DAY.

Max hangs up his jacket. Passes to the room. Catches Irina's waiting glance.

MAX
I think that Vasya and Yulya will
have a whirlwind romance and lots
of discoveries ... (he smiles))

EPISODE 41 INT. MAX'S OFFICE/BCS OFFICE. DAY/EVENING.

Cut-ins (3-7 seconds each):
Jeep with money. (Max took money from different places and people, Slava was driving)
Shares - shareholders - reports that Bykov put on Shelikhovsky's table.
Money-shares-report on Shelikhovsky's table.

CHAPTER 3. REMUNERATION.

EPISODE 42 INT. MAX'S OFFICE / BCS OFFICE.DAY

BYKOV
(by phone) Prepared two papers
for the director. One about you,
the other about friends. Here -
the work of professionals. And
they fucked people up ... And
here - friends - all honest, but
the turnover is 30 times lower,
and the average purchase price is

higher. He was amazed. They rolled up activities.

MAX

I heard nothing new for myself. I'm more interested in the question, when we will get the salary, finally. Show the numbers!

BYKOV

Soon, soon. Aren't you afraid?

MAKC

I have not been afraid of anything for a long time.

EPISODE 43 INT. BCS OFFICE/MAX'S OFFICE. DAY

Max is standing at the table with a handset in his hand.

MAX

Enough, I'm tired of waiting! Give me my paycheck!

BYKOV

I'll drop by the other day. Tell us how much we owe you. We have not seen the money ourselves.

MAX

Counted. Sales prices I took at minimum level: 70 - Azot, 2.7 - Kuzbassenergo. Including the Large client and the whole national package ... We could not fuck on the national package! Total - 30%: 1,223,532 rubles.

Pause

BYKOV

I'll drop by tomorrow.

MAX

Waiting for you.

EPISODE 44 INT. MAX'S OFFICE. SAME DAY.

MAX
(Hangs up
looking at Vasilyev) We are
waiting.

VASILYEV
Do you really think they will
give us this amount of money?

MAX
If they give, then for such
conversations, I will impose a
fine on you.

VASILIEV
(getting up from the table) Who
made me speak ...

MAX
We are out of money. All papers are in the
registry. No trumps.

EPISODE 45 INT. MAX'S OFFICE. DAY

FIRST PAYCHECK

Bykov, standing near the table, takes out a file with papers out of the case.

BYKOV
Here are the calculations.
(pushes documents towards Max)
Can we can talk face to face (in
a quiet voice, so that Vasiliev
does not hear).

MAX
((without looking at the documents, he shakes his head)
Tell me - how much?

Pause.

BYKOV
300,000 - 10% and I only have 100,000 on me... They cropped as much as they could ...

MAX
(pushes documents away from you)
Take it ... I'm not interested in looking at it.

Picks up, dials

MAX
Vitaly, why so little?

VOICE OF SHELIKHOVSKY
Like so.

Max hangs up without saying a word.

MAX
How mad I am.

BYKOV
Will you go and sort it out, really?
(turning his head to Vasilyev)
Volodya, go get some vodka with a snack.

EPISODE 46 INT. MAX'S OFFICE. SAME DAY.

Bykov, Max and Vasilyev are sitting at the table. Dark, oppressive silence. The bottle is finished

BYKOV
Beat the fuck out of me! Or go beat the fuck out of him...
(shuddering)

MAX
Alexey... There are more important things in life, than money. Give me this hundred.

Bykov pulls out of the bag 100,000 and gives them to Murashka, Murashka throws fifty thousands on the table.

MAX(TO VOLODYA)
Your half. You were right.

Vasilyev quickly grabs the money.

Pause

MAXC
(to Bykov) Buy from us... Now! 100,000 KE, at a stock price of 3.5.

Bykov dials Shelikhovsky's number.

BYKOV
They offer to buy 100,000 Kuzbassenergo from them at the stock exchange price... (they hear from the handset: oh, flip them off ... But ...) Ok. Bought ..

MAX
So what? The paycheck depends on the mood of the director?

BYKOV
Yeah... Depends on the mood of the director.

Transfer.

Bykov is about to leave.

BYKOV
If I were you, I would have signed the paper then.

Max doesn't respond.

After Bykov left.

MAX
We'll get our own back… What do we have between us?

VASILYEV
Shares plus cash. 1.5 million rubles.

MAX
I'll buy a flat and do repair. Enough to live with parents.

VASILYEV
I will buy an apartment for my wife's parents, I will return the debt, enough to live with parents.

MAX
(nods silently) Listen to my order. Fuck on all fronts!

VASILYEV
Clear.

EPISODE 47 NATURE. PARK/ IN THE STREET. DAY.

Max and Irina are walking down the street.

MAX
Irina, I bought an apartment. Ask Vasya if he agrees to do repairs. And maybe he will forgive me, finally ...

IRINA
I'll ask him. You surprised us with your apartment.

CHAPTER 4.9/11.

EPISODE 48 INT. MAX'S OFFICE. DAY.

Max and Irina work in the office - they fill out papers. Vasilyev enters the office.

VASILYEV
I tooke the shares to the register.

MAX
News. Bykov is up to something different. We keep in touch via Slava.

VASILIEV
News. There was a scandal in the registry of Azot, the registrar leaves, looking for a replacement. Asked for a man from us.

Pause

Murashka dials the registrar.

MAX
Good afternoon. Do you need an employee?

REGISTRAR
Yes, we do.

MAX
(looking at Irina) There is such a person. Her name is Irina, she graduated from the faculty of romance and germanic philology with honours, perfectly knows English, responsible and if it goes well, I will add you some money...

REGISTRAR
Let her come.

Max hangs up. Turns to Irina smiling.

MAX
Congratulations, now you have a job. In addition to salary, you will also buy shares. Now you are Azot's registrar!

VASILYEV
All power to the Soviets! Now we have Azot register.

EPISODE 49 INT. MAX'S OFFICE. SAME DAY.

The door of the office closes behind Irina's back.

MAX
(to Vasilyev) Now we also have a back office - cost savings. Interaction with Irina is completely on you. (Eye contact with Vasilyev) I decided to take a pause in a personal relationship with her.

Vasilyev nods silently.

EPISODE 50 INT.MAX'S OFFICE/BCS OFFICE.DAY.

JUNE

Max calls to BCS.

MAX
Slava, call Irina, she will provide you with the report.

Max hangs up. He turns to Vasilyev who is standing at the window, covering the receiver with his hand..

MAX
How do we fuck them?

VASILYEV
In all ways possible!

SLAVA'S VOICE IN THE RECEIVER
We do not trust you.

MAX
Oh, it's you who don't trust us? Show us the numbers...

SHILOV
(stretching the words mockingly)
A company within a company.

EPISODE 51

Chronicle cut-ins: stock exchange, stocks, news front pages.

EPISODE 52 INT. MAX'S OFFICE. DAY.

Phone is ringing. Max picks up.

FINANCIAL ALLIANCE
What are you doing !? Put your person in the register…! We will write a complaint to the FCSM..

MAX
One moment(with artificial surprise), I'll call Irina... to tell her you are happy.

He drops call and dials a number.

MAX
Irina, the Alliance called, said that I put my person ... They will write a complaint to the FCSM on us …

IRINA
(after a moment) If I hear such rudeness again, I will not accept more documents from them.

EPISODE 53 INT. MAX'S OFFICE.DAY.

NEGOTIATIONS
City streets. The flow of cars. Hurrying pedestrians. Buyers at street kiosks.

MAX
(To Vasilyev) I got 1.5. Put the papers in archive, you can spend 600,000, the rest is in deposit box. I will beat up our salary...

VASILYEV
Are we blocking the purchase?

Max nods.

VASILYEV
Clear.

Phone is ringing.

MAX (TO SHILOV)
Yes, I got 1.5. Four months has passed, do us a favour and pay for our work. We refuse from working for 10%, we need 30%.

SLAVA
We have settled it.

MAX
We have been settling, but we haven't settled it...

SLAVA
A question to Vitaly (switches to Shelikhovsky)

Pause.

SHELIKHOVSKY
What were the last words by Bykov?

MAX
Depends on the director's mood...

SHELIKHOVSKY
(grinning)I'll do and ask the director about his mood.

MAX
Closer to the topic, please.

SHELIKHOVSKY
30% is ok with us.

MAX
20%

Pause.

SHELIKHOVSKY
Come to our office.

Max hangs up. Quickly does calculations.

MAX
(to Vasilyev) turnover is down, low season... 20% of the profit is around 260,000.

EPISODE 54 INT. BCS OFFICE. DAY.

Max is sitting at the table in the BCS canteen.

SHELIKHOVSKY
(Shelikhovsky runs into the room)
And how much of my money do you keep...

Pause.

(continues)
(looking aside) He'll tell he took it from me…

Max shakes his hand.

SHELIKHOVSKY
Go to the backoffice and get the money.

EPISODE 55 INT. MAX'S OFFICE. DAY.

IRINA GOES TO NOVOSIBIRSK TO STUDY

Max comes in and sees Vasilyev pouring coffee.

MAX
265,000

VASILYEV
OK.

VASILYEV
Irina passed the probationary period. The registry holder sends her to Novosibirsk, to study, to obtain a registrar certificate.

MAX
Great.

VASILYEV
One more thing. (a quick glance on Max)... She talked with Slava while I was there and asked him to meet her at the station.

Pause.

MAX

When does she leave?

VASILYEV

On the 9th, for 10 days.

MAX

(slowly, pausing between) Today is 7th. We go on vacation as of tomorrow. Until my further order.

VASILYEV

Clear.

EPISODE 56 NAT/INT NOVOSIBIRSK.

Irina is in Novosibirsk.

Cut-ins (10-15 seconds each):
Inside a new jeep
Restaurants
Well-lit night streets

Frank erotic scene - Irina and Slava.

EPISODE 57 INT. MAX'S APARTMENT. EVENING.

9/11

Max - in his apartment, lying on a mattress, in front of the TV, looking at repeated footage of the collapse of skyscrapers.

Phone is ringing.

SLAVA

Hi.

MAX

Hi. How awful! (he still looks at the screen)

SLAVA
You have losses.

MAX
Where?

SLAVA
From the last 100,000, so what are we goiing to do?

MAX
We take responsibility even for our losses. 20% is 20,000. Pieve of cake... We'll work it off.

SLAVA
And one more thing. Shelikhovsky asks you to continue your work.

An excitedly screaming American television reporter (Russian television news release) is on the screen, behind which is a wall of smoke and running people ... Fire trucks.

EPISODE 58

Short cut-ins (3-5 seconds):
Max is alone: on the streets, in a cafe, lying on the sofa / mattress at home in front of the TV. He is clearly trying to make some sort of decision for himself.

EPISODE 59 INT. MAX'S OFFICE. DAY.

Max and Vasiliev return to work. Max dials the number.

MAX
(to Slava)
We got bored and decided to return to work.

SLAVA
(grinning)why did you get bored?

Max hangs up without saying a word.

VASILYEV
Irina has arrived. She will drop by in the evening.

EPISODE 60 INT MAX'S OFFICE. EVENING.

IRINA'S COMEBACK, "HOT" MEETING

Irina comes into the office.

VASILYEV
How was your trip?

IRINA
Great, it was interesting. It was my first time in Novosibirsk.

MAX
What about BCS? Have you been recruited?

Silence.

MAX
Let's go to my place and talk.

IRINA
Let's go.

Transition.
Max and Irina silently ride in a taxi.

At some point, Irina obviously wants to say something, but Max shakes his head and makes the music louder (a song that is playing should reflect the situation).

EPISODE 61 INT. MAX'S APARTMENT. EVENING.

Max and Irina silently take off their outer clothing and pass into the room - Irina goes first. Max stops in the doorway, looks at the girl.

Max stays in the room. Irina goes out on the balcony, talking with Max standing with her back to him.

MAX
You have changed a lot... Has something happened?

IRINA
I met a guy.

Irina goes inside the room and comes to Max.

MAX
And what is his name?

Pause. Max approaches Irina.

MAX
I repeat my question - name!!!

Pause.

IRINA
Slava.

MAX
You've been used!

Max slaps Irina on the cheek with his palm. Irina, clutching her cheek, retreats from Max. She comes up to her and hits with the back of his hand over the open cheek. Irina retreats another step. She wants to bypass Max, but he grabs her hand - and gives another slap in the face ... More, and more ... Irina covers her face with her palms ...

MAX
I'll see you off to your house. Tomorrow we will continue the conversation.

EPISODE 62 NAT. STREETS OF THE CITY. EVENING.

Max meets Irina after work. They walk along the street, go to the supermarket. They go outside.

MAX
Let's go to my place.

Irina nods subtly, looking to the opposite direction.

EPISODE 63 INT. MAX'S APARTMENT. EVENING. THE OTHER DAY.

Max and Irina are lying on the matress after having sex.

MAX
I haven't experienced such passion for a long time.

IRINA
I understand...

MAX
Does Slava know that I beat you?

IRINA
Yes, we talked. He asked: what if youfight with him?

MAX
Let him beat me first. Now tell me more about the trip...

IRINA
It happened on the first day. We were sitting in a restaurant, he invited me to his place. I replied that I agreed that everything should have happened that way.
Riding through the night Novosibirsk in a jeep ....

MAX
Where did Slava take the jeep?

IRINA
It's Shelikhovsky's jeep. We have been dating for the whole week.

MAX
(sarcastically) Poor Slava.

IRINA
Probably, it was all the same as with you. We went to the bookstore, I advised him interesting books. He asked if you read them.

MAX
What did you answer?

IRINA
I said that Max read the main ones. He noted that we were only talking about work.

MAX
Where did you have your meetings?

IRINA
In one of Shelikhovsky's apartments. He lives there with his mom.

MAX
With Shelikhovksy's mom!? Tell me more about her.

IRINA
She advised Slava to marry me. She liked me.

MAX
What else?

IRINA
Currently not married. She had several husbands. She worked as a chief accountant in the Sakhalin fleet. She smokes, drinks. Once she brought a man, they sat all night, talking in the kitchen. She worships Vitaly. Shelikhovsky's father was the captain of the ship. She is not very good with Svetlana Shelikhovskaya.

MAX
Svetlana Shelikhovskaya?! His wife! What can you tell about her?

IRINA
Not much about her. I've seen her once from afar, she works in BCS together with Vitaly and they

have conflicts... Because of him cheating on her.

MAX
Interesting... What else?

IRINA
Slava wanted to introduce me to Vitaly, but for some reason the meeting did not take place. And when I was leaving back at the station, he asked me - for how much you actually buy shares..

MAX
Clear. When are you back to Novosibirsk?

IRINA
Ia a week. I'll have my exam to obtain certificate.

MAX
I am proposing you. (slightly squinting his eyes, looking at Irina's puzzled expression on his face). Marry me.

Pause.

IRINA
I'll go to Novosibirsk first.

She throws a glance at Max.

(she continues)
I need to think. (Abruptly sits up in bed, sitting with her back to Max) And also, Slava said that I might get a job there.

MAX
I'll remember that.

EPISODE 64 INT. MAX'S OFFICE. DAY.

Max calls BCS.

MAX

(To Slava)Call back to Irina, she will provide you with the report. And one more thing, I proposed her.

Silence. Max hangs up. Looks at Vasilyev.

VASILYEV

I don't know what to say (shakes his head).

MAX

(to Volodya) In a week Irina goes to the exam. These days you will work alone. The answer to the question - "where did Murashka go?" is Murashka has a binge. If she does not return, I will have to leave.

VASILYEV

Clear.

EPISODE 65 INT/NAT "TENDERLOINS OF KEMEROVO".

Short cut-ins: Max and Irina in restaurants, etc.

A transition to episode 66 from one of the restaurants' doors.

EPISODE 66 INT. RESTAURANT.EVENING

Max and Irina in a restaurant.

Max stares at her.

IRINA

(distictly nervous under his stare) **I'll say no to both!**

MAX
Listen, it's worth a lot now. You come to Novosibirsk and say to Slava: he slept with my sister, I slept with you, we are even. Listen to what he'll respond. And no sex! Otherwise - I can not get you or myself out of it.

IRINA
Aren't you afraid?

MAX
I am no longer afraid of anything.

EPISODE 67 NAT. NOVOSIBIRSK. DAY/EVENING.

In short cut-ins:

Irina in Novosibirsk: with Julia. At the exam. In the city.

EPISODE 68 INT. MAX'S APARTMENT. EVENING.

IRINA'S RETURN, "WARM" MEETING

A knock on the door. Irina is at the doorway.

MAX
Come in...

Rumpled from a hangover, Max gets a bottle of vodka.

MAX
Let's have a drink first.

IRINA
Let's celebrate my certificate.

They have a drink.

MAX
And now tell me in a soft and quiet voice...

IRINA
What you want to know... We had no sex.

Max does not hide a sigh of relief.

MAX
Tell me about your trip.

IRINA
We went with Julia, she wanted to look at him, she did not like him. We went to a restaurant, where he burst out, said all sorts of nonsense. I did not hear any proposals. And another interesting point. Once he came to visit me and Julia in the hotel, brought food, and after he left, two guys knocked and asked if we asked for a company 'Leisuretime'...

MAX
It's clean and clear to me. Come and stay with me.

EPISODE 69 INT. MAX'S OFFICE. MORNING.

Max enters the office. Silently greets Vasilyev. Undresses, notices that Vasilyev looks at him questioningly.

MAX
It has passed. We continue to buy.

VASILYEV
(with ease) Clear.

Max dials the number. Slava picks up.

MAX
So how am going to report to you now?

Pause.

SLAVA
I'll switch to BYKOV now.

BYKOV
(silently) Shelikhovsky got fucked. Who fucked him? Maxim Murashka - a buyer from Kemerovo.
So what do we have?
Slava was under Shelikhovsky.
Max was under Shelikhovsky.
Irina was under Max. But her sister?
That's us who got used! And like whom? Like fucking fuckers. Why haven't you fucked her for 2 months? But a wife? They'l say - he sold his wife. You'd better fucked.

MAX
I'm impressed by your awareness. We continue buying.

BYKOV
Who did they want to fuck? I quit. Bonus is 300 thousand. A bone thrown. BCS employees are paid pennies..

EPISODE 70

5-6 seconds cut-ins (Bykov's departure):
He collects things from the desktop (can be in the American style - in the box), gets money at the cashier's.

CHAPTER 5. GENTLEMEN'S AGREEMENT.

EPISODE 71 INT. MAX'S OFFICE/BCS OFFICE. DAY.

SVETLANA SHELIKHOVSKAYA, GENTLEMEN'S AGREEMENT

Phone is ringing. Max hangs up.

(A PLEASANT FEMALE VOICE)
Svetlana Shelikhovskaya. Keep in touch via me now.

MAX
Nice to meet you. Things are shaping up. We bought 100,000 more shares of KE, there's 10% profit, sell it.

SVETLANA
I cannot sell, It's Shelikhovsky who is in charge.

MAX
Clear.

EPISODE 72 INT. MAX'S OFFICE. SAME DAY.

May hangs up.

VASILYEV
Svetlana Shelikhovskaya!?

MAX
Yep.

Max gets up from the table, walks to the window. Looking out into the street, he is silent for a few seconds. Then he turns to Vasilyev

(continues)
Listen to my order - We stop fucking!

VASILYEV
(distrustfully) At all?! Not even a bit?!

MAX

Not even a bit. We'll buy some more for the report and off to Novosibirsk.

EPISODE 73

Max's way to Novosibirsk - in cut-ins. He enters the BCS office.

EPISODE 74 INT. BCS OFFICE. DAY.

Shelikhovsky is standing at the window. Max is sitting at the table. Svetlana is sitting opposite to him.

SHELIKHOVSKY

So it was Irina who fucked Slava, and Slava is the guy!

Max keeps silent, unzipping the bag.

SHELIKHOVSKY

He should have made a proposal. Then we would have replayed it all...

Moves from the window, sits at the table.

(continues looking at Max)

If the director fucked Svetlana, I would also beat the shit out of her.

Max shakes his head, listening to Shelikhovsky's tirade.

SHELIKHOVSKY

Who am I working with...

Max pulls a report out of his bag and puts it on the table in front of Shelikhovsky, pointing his finger at him.

MAX

With this report, I propose to conclude a gentleman's agreement. You understand me ... And from now on, I will tell myself when to sell ... We must also have the

right to sell our papers 2-3 times a year, to sell our papers at the exchange price.

SHELIKHOVSKY
Just, please, no scandals. That is - you will not fuck Svetlana. Let's go to the restaurant. Svetlana will go with us.

SVETLANA
Gentlemen's agreement is not an economic term.

SHELIKHOVSKY
Do you want to be fucked up?

MAX
Chicago clean hand rule.

Silence.

EPISODE 75 INT. RESTAURANT. EVENING.

The restaurant has few visitors (expensive restaurant), music is playing softly.

SVETLANA
Vitaly, this girl who was appointed head of the department - who is cooler me or her?

MAX
Svetlana, of course, you are! You're Shelikhovsky's wife!

Svetlana grins, looking at her husband, and then at Max.

MAX

(changing his voice to a dryer one) Slava and Ira... Such a resonance! Vitaly, our moms are alike. The only thing different is that my mom had one husband. Dominant mother is a classical story.

Pause

SVETLANA

How do you know Vitaly's mom?

Max keeps silent, as if haven't heard the question.

(continues - realizing that there will be no answer)
And who are your parents?

MAX

My father worked as a dispatcher in the management of heating networks, Kuzbassenergo. Mother was head of the children's department of the dental clinic. There is nothing to be proud of. Father was on bad terms with his chief. Apparently, I have inherited this way of life.

SHELIKHOVSKY

We are sitting ... (drinking beer, drank beer) (to Svetlana) Of course - how will he negotiate for Kuzbassenergo ... (for Kuzbassenergo’s forced buyout - one notary was put in prison, the second was removed from his post, the third is in question. They squeezed a bribe from what Murashka inherited from his father, the BCS was engaged in the re-registration of rights)

MAX

I am having a creative block at the moment.

SHELIKHOVSKY
(to Svetlana) He doesn't know how to fuck it up. We have people working for a 3% fee...

SVETLANA
Mom is head ... Why is it nothing? You have to be proud, it's parents. . .

MAX
What does it mean (emphasizing the word "have to") have to be proud of? You are either proud, or not.

SHELIKHOVSKY
I agree ... (nodding slightly at Svetlana) She was just more lucky with her parents. So you have healthy teeth, don't you?

MAX
Yes, all of them. And I tell everyone: you can wear ragged clothes, but you cannot neglect your teeth.

SHELIKHOVSKY
And I need to have one tooth attended here. (pointing to the tooth with a finger)

SVETLANA
What education do you have?

MAX
Graduated with honors from the Medical Academy. I was interested in the mechanisms of the development of diseases most of all.

SVETLANA
And we are mathematicians - physicists.

MAX
Vitaly has a strong defense and no guilt at all.

SVETLANA
(smiling) What you say about guilt is right.

SHELIKHOVSKY
(turning to Sveta) I told you. (making a vague gesture with his hand) I defend from them ...

SVETLANA
(staring at Max) Have you watched 'One Flew over the Cuckoo's Nest'?

MAX
The movie is not so great. You need to read a book.

SVETLANA
And have you read it?

MAX
Yes, I have.

(Svetlana, slightly shaking her head)

SHELIKHOVSKY
We had a nice evening, let's go home.

EPISODE 76 NAT. IN THE STREET/PARK. DAY.

NO WEDDING

Irina and Max are walking down the street. Not far away is the building of the registry office.

IRINA
I woke up! Is it really so?

MAX
So now you understand what love is?

IRINA
Yes, a bruised ego.

MAX
Now you are probably thinking - how good would it have been with Slava,had he behaved otherwise?

IRINA
More or less like that.

MAX
How many men have you had during this period, apart from him?

IRINA
Two more. Maybe you should think of changing the job?

MAX
Everywhere is the same thing ... That's interesting - now you understand that it is useless to lie to me. How do you see our family, ideally?

IRINA
Ideally? Ideally - I play around. But I love only you. But you will not forgive me for Slava, and I will not forgive you for my sister.

MAX
(shaking his head) I am one of those men who can not be cheated on. What about children?

IRINA
I do not want to have them.

Max stops. Irina, having made one more step, also stops, turning to Max with a puzzled expression on her face.

MAX
(staring at Irina) You can leave. At your convenience.

Pause.

IRINA
(silently) and what about your proposal?

She looks at the registry office, then back to Max.

MAX
I give up on it.

IRINA
(lost, casting a glance at Max, who is looking somewhere up ahead) I will not be able to return home.

MAX
It's for the best. We will not let you die of hunger and will try to preserve friendship. We can always talk.

Max goes forward ... Irina slows down her steps. Stops looking after Max.

EPISODE 77 INT. BCS OFFICE. DAY.

Max enters Shelikhovsky's office.
Silently sits at the table.
Max and Shelikhovsky look at each other.
Svetlana enters the office.

SVETLANA
Million

Max and Shelikhovsky continue to look at each other in silence.

Svetlana leaves the office.

Max and Shelikhovsky still silently look at each other.
Max abruptly gets up from the table and leaves the office, slamming the door.

Shelikhovsky peeks out of the office and sees that Max is walking towards the toilet.

Transition:
Max smokes in the toilet

Max returns to the office. He remains to stand next to the table.

SHELIKHOVSKY
I will call the security guys now.

Pause

You definitely do not fuck.

MAX
250 gran and I go the fuck out of here.

SHELIKHOVSKY
Take 200.

Max silently leaves the office.
Cut-ins (3-4 seconds):
He goes through the corridors of the BCS. Goes outside. Goes mingling with a crowd of passers-by.

EPISODE 78 INT. MAX'S OFFICE. DAY.

Max is sitting at the table. Vasilyev, with a cup of coffee in his hand, is standing by the window.

MAX
Do you understand the meaning of my last order? Not to fuck them up.

VASILYEV
It's not my usual way of working.

MAX
All operations are under my control now. Or you have forgotten 9/11?

VASILYEV
No, I haven't.

Knock on the door. The door opens slightly and we see head of Vasily. Max nods and Vasily enters the office.

MAX
(to Vasilyev) I take Vasya to work. He will perform technical tasks. We are no longer coping.

VASILYEV
(shrugging) Clear.

MAX
Congratulations, Vasily! Now you are a cool trader. The bathroom that you made to me shook me to the depths of my soul (smiling), but first you need to change the holey shoes.

VASYA
What am I to do?

MAX
Fill out papers and bring money to work.

VASYA
How much money to bring?

MAX
1.5 - 2.5 mln.(smiling).

VASYA
This is not the money to steal.

MAX
That's a comfort. (noticing that Vasily clearly wants to say something). What else?

VASYA
Irina is going to live at my place.

MAX
No sex?

VASYA
Of course, we are friends.

MAX
I believe you.

EPISODE 79 INT. MAX'S OFFICE. DAY.

We see the text of the e-mail on the monitor screen.
Max sends an e-mail Shelikhovsky saying that there will be no wedding.

EPISODE 80 INT. BCS OFFICE. DAY.

FEBRUARY, 23, WHY HAVEN'T YOU GOT MARRIED?

Max comes to the BCS office. Enters Svetlana's office.

MAX
Hello. Here's the report.

SVETLANA
Hi. We are celebrating today. Are you gonna stay?

MAX
Yes, I am.

SVETLANA
Have you served in the army?

MAX
No, I am lieutenant of the reserve of the medical service.

EPISODE 81 INT. BCS OFFICE. DAY.

"Kitchen" zone at BCS. Tables with snacks and drinks. The staff comes and presents gift. Max feels stranger among the guests, all sounds go like a background to his state of mind. While there is a distribution of gifts, he is happy to eat and drink.

(behind the scenes)
SILENT FEMALE VOICE
And Vas'ka listens and eats
......

EPISODE 82 INT. BCS OFFICE. EVENING.

The following are on the "stage" (part of the hall): supervisor, head of analytical department, head of the training center and Max.

Max immediately realized from the poem, they began to read, that they were talking about him and began to show "star gestures."
Upon reading of the poem, Max is given a gift - two cheap glasses.

Can’t Maksim abuse his name,
He isn’t placed within the frame.
He’ll achieve all his success
Without any embarrassments.
Can become he celebrated
Either actor, either bandit.
He becomes musician famous,
Even Mozart will be jealous.
God forbid, a war descends,
He will lead the battalions.
If Max finishes a treatise,
He’ll be awarded the Nobel Prize.
With such miraculous name
You are just Achillean.
During lifetime make headway -
Oh, the Name, don’t give away.

Vitaly and Svetlana watched the action a little bit far away. Director General of BCS ran past to his office. His door gives into the "kitchen"..

Max is standing at the table, holding the gift in an armpit. He is uncomfortable - he shows to the employee of the BCS standing in front of him to take a gift and put it next to him in the free space. The employee freezes fearfully, as if he had to do something very complicated and, with his eyes slightly squinted, looks somewhere away from Max. Turning his head slightly, Max sees that the employee is looking at Shelikhovsky.

EPISODE 83 INT. BCS OFFICE. EVENING.

Cut-ins: 5-7 seconds

Two girls pull Max away from the table, laughing, pulling him into a place in the "kitchen", forcing him to participate in the contest.

Contest is to inflate condoms, with drawing women's fillet part on them.
Max takes an active part in the competition, but drops the condom on the floor ...

MAX
I do not use them...

He examines what other participants created with addiction. A group of girls, around 10, watch the process with interest.

(a voice of a participant - Shein)
MALE VOICE
Boobs and butt, are they considered to be a woman?

MALE VOICE
You are wrong...

EPISODE 84 INT. BCS OFFICE. LATE EVENING.

In Shelikhovsky's office. Drunk Max and Vitaly.

SHELIKHOVSKY
Why haven't you got married?

MAX
I have a problem with her personal views on life.

SHELIKHOVSKY
Let's go to the bar.

Chapter 6. CAREER GROWTH.

EPISODE 85 INT. MAX'S NEW OFFICE. MORNING.

FAREWELL TO THE PAST

Max drives up to a new modern building, which houses his new office.

The phone rings continuously.

MAX
(to Vasiliev) We were rewarded for good and honest work. Now we are representatives of BCS. We can provide a full range of services. Keep in touch via Shelikhovsky.

VASILYEV
(nods without emotion) There's no sense in these services. Buying is our bread. Azot has lost interest towards it. It is necessary to pour off ours (inquiringly looks at Max)..

MAX
I'll pour it off. You've invested the main part of it in the real estate. I will be pouring off. What do we have?

VASILYEV
Shares and money, that's 7 million. One more thing, Irina is getting fired. The register is transferred to another person.

Partners' eyes meet.
Pause.

MAX
Let her come in tomorrow.

EPISODE 86 INT.MAX'S OFFICE. DAY

Irina and Max are at Max's office.

IRINA
I don't know what to do...

MAX
I've an idea. Ask BCS...

IRINA
How? After all that happened?

MAX
That was nothing... I even know what you will tell tomoroow when you enter her after talking to BCS...

EPISODE 87 INT. MAX'S OFFICE. DAY

Irina is at the office in Kemerovo.

IRINA
(happily) They employ me as translator, BCS! (she adds quickly) And let it be like this - it's Me who dumped you.

MAX
Good. Only, what's the show-off for again? (Shakes his head) My prediction is 3 months. Then you get fired.

IRINA
We'll see. I am preparing for leaving.

MAX
I do not give you any more instructions.

EPISODE 88 INT. BCS OFFICE/MAX'S OFFICE. SAME DAY

Shelikhovsky's ringing.

SHELIKHOVSKY
We want to hire Irina as a translator. Usually we entrust this work to third parties. And now we thought that we'd better

have our own one. What's your
opinion?

MAX
It's up to you.

EPISODE 89 INT/NAT

3-5 seconds cut-ins

Max puts a stack of documents (report) in the bag.
Max and Vasily get in the car.
The car rides through the streets of the city, going to the countryside ...
The pointer flashes: "Novosibirsk"
They go changing places - taking turns at the wheel

EPISODE 90 INT. IRINA'S APARTMENT/BCS OFFICE. EVENING/MORNING.

Max's car stops near the house where Irina lives.

Max and Vasily enter Irina's apartment.

MAX

So, you live here…

IRINA

(shrugging) For now. Shelikhovsky gave me this apartment for a start.

MAX
Let him
prepare the money. We'll
arrive at the office closer
to the lunchtime.

TRANSITION - BCS OFFICE.MORNING

SHELIKHOVSKY
(smirking) How was your night?
Oh, you came with Vasily.

Max shakes his head.

Max and Vasily walk down the corridor. Irina goes towards them, stops. Max stops near. Silently he makes a move with a nod - "Did you want something?"

IRINA
Why are you **like that**?

Questioning expression on Max's face - he shrugs.

MAX
Like what?

IRINA
Apart from business... Not a word...

VASYA

(surprisingly) And it's you ask - why is he **like that**?

Max leaves the corridor. After hesitating for a second, Vasily glances at Irina and follows him. Svetlana comes out of the office, walks up to Vasily.

SVETLANA
You have to let it go.

Vasily shrugs and follows Max.

CHAPTER 7. WEDDING. CHANGES.

EPISODE 91 INT. CANTEEN. DAY.

MURASHKA'S WEDDING, COUNTERSTRIKE

The canteen, where Max and Vasily usually dine. Max pays attention to a pretty girl.

Max walks over to a girl who was about to leave.

MAX
Let me introduce myself - Maxim Murashka.

GIRL
(slightly surprised) Natalya Staroseltseva.

MAX
Come to my office at any suitable time...

NATALYA
I will come.

EPISODE 92 INT. MAX'S OFFICE. SAME DAY.

Max looks at the girl who came in.

MAX
Natalya, could you, please, turn around ...

Natalia turns around, makes several elegant movements.

MAX
(talking to Vasily) How is she?

VASILY
Cool!!!

MAKC
(to Natalys) Marry me.

NATALYA
I'll think about it...

EPISODE 93 INT/NAT.

WEDDING

Fragments of wedding - 3-5 second cut-ins

EPISODE 94 INT. MAX'S APARTMENT. MORNING.

The apartment is slightly messy after celebrations.

MAX
A trip? To Marmaris?

NATALYS
Superb!

MAX
And when we are back, we'll drop by at the BCS office. And we want wait long to have a child.

EPISODE 95 INT. BCS OFFICE.DAY.

Tanned and relaxed Max and Natalya are walking along the BCS office. Everybody looks at them.

Max walks around BCS. You can hear muffled remarks all around - some of the phrases are said so that Max or Natalya (she was standing in the corner in the kitchen) heard them.

COME, COME AND SEE THIS -
(Mintsev, friendly)(a small, fat,
lame bespectacled guy)
DID HE GET MARRIED ON PURPOSE - F
voice
DID SHE UNDERSTAND WHOM SHE
MARRIED - F voice
THAT'S HOW YOU GET SOLD, AND YOU
WON'T EVEN REALIZE - F voice BUT
THAT'S WIFE - F voice (there was
a girl from the street who was
taken by a guy before me)
WE HIRED A NON-PROFESSIONAL HERE,
AND LOOK WHAT WE'VE GOT... - F
voice
AND WHAT DO YOU WANT? ANYWAY... f
voice
WITH OUR OWN WEAPON f voice
WHAT ARE YOU SAYING? - f voice
SOLD A WHORE? WHERE? WHAT WHORE?
OH, THERE SHE GOES...VITALY
WOULDN'T BE ABLE TO OVERCOME THIS
- m voice
AS IF HE IS LILY-WHITE - f voice
AND WHAT ABOUT WIFE? SHE'LL TELL
WHAT THE FUCK DID WE GO TO
MARMARIS (Shelikhovsky)
WOULD YOU LIKE TO WORK IN BCS? -
m voice
AREN'T YOU ASHAMED? PEOPLE TAKE
SUCH A GREAT RESPONSIBILITY HERE
- f voice
At Shelikhovsky's office.
LET'S GIVE HIM MONEY - f voice
HE'LL TAKE MONEY AND LEAVE -
Shelikhovsky.
HERE, WHAT WE'VE GOT... - f voice
WE UNDERESTIMATED YOU - m voice
YOU TOOK A WHORE, AND YOU DON'T
TAKE HIM? - f voice
YOU'LL NEED TO FUCK HERE. - f
voice
IT WON'T LAST LONG BASED ON FEAR
- f voice
M makes a gesture: punch in the
palm, on the opposite side.

MAX (to a random
girl in Irina's office)
And how did you get to BCS?

Girl (shuddering)
Via employment office.

Natalia does not understand anything.
At some point, she is left alone in the kitchen. Employees of the BCS pass by her, sometimes joining groups of 3-4 people, casting glances at her - as if offering themselves for her to choose.

Pale, collapsed, plump Irina. Seeing Max with Natalya, she leaves immediately.

EPISODE 96 INT. BCS OFFICE. DAY.

Max meets Svetlana in the BCS canteen.

SVETLANA
Where did you go?

MAX
(head down guiltily): To Marmaris.

SVETLANA
(shakes her head) Hang the architect ...
Vitaly was caught at the woman ... Believe it or not? Vitaly was faked out. You would have felt sorry for him ...
He will say - who would have sorry for me.

Max shakes his head.

(continues) Now you've changed places.
By the way, branches now have 30%, minus expenses. Up to plus infinity. It is working...
I do not know this girl ...

Murashka shakes his head.

EPISODE 97 INT. SHELIKHOVSKY'S OFFICE.DAY

SHELIKHOVSKY
I have this (shows one finger), only one is possible here...

MAX
And I have this (haughtily) (showing two fingers, Victoria). I propose to fix the profit for the last volume. **It is working...**

SHELIKHOVSKY
Up to plus infinity... Ok. It's well thought over. Fucked me again.

MAX
The best of the bum-fuckers. (leaving the office, to himself.)

EPISODE 98 INT. MAX'S OFFICE. DAY.

Max walks quickly down the hall. Concentrated, as if ready to take some important decision. Enters the office. Glances at Vasilyev.

VASILYEV
What happened?

MAX
Storm on the horizon.

MAX
(calling to Shelikhovsky) Pour off all Kuzbassenergo shares.

SHELIKHOVSKY
(after a short pause) I am selling all.

CHAPTER 8. YUKOS CASE. LEAVING.

EPISODE 99

Chronicles and papers. Yukos case.

EPISODE 100 INT. BCS OFFICE/MAX'S OFFICE. DAY.

Phone rings at Max's office. He picks up.

SHELIKHOVSKY
We stop buying, what's the situation?

MAX
The price is fixed... At the lowest profitable level. I purchased 3,000 Azot shares

SHELIKHOVSKY
And where are these from?

MAX
There are none. Azaot is panicking. The register does not work, it passes on to others. The competitors fell silent. Panic all around. We buy 70% cheaper than the stock exchange price.

SHELIKHOVSKY
Ok. Bye.

MAX
Wait. Have you poured off all Kuzbassenergo shares?

SHELIKHOVSKY
All. You definitely have 30%. The director does not know, what to do with his 2,000,000.

MAX
(with ease): Perfect.

EPISODE 101 MAX'S OFFICE.

Phone rings at Max's office.

SHELIKHOVSKY
You are **fined** for
the delay of Azot's delivery.

MAX
The price remained below the exchange. The volume is large, we started as quickly as we could. I am asking for the document..

SHELIKHOVSKY
The document?... You'll get the one with fines.

Max hangs up. The document with fines comes by fax.

Buying shares in Max's office - shareholder - money - shareholder - money.

The phone rings.

SHELIKHOVSKY
I sold out Azot.

MAX
All Azot shares are sold?

SHELIKHOVSKY
All.

MAX
At a presumably lower price.

Short pause. (continues)

MAX
I decided to leave.

Pause

SHELIKHOVSKY
Come to my office.

The hour hand of the wall clock takes several turns.

Call from BCS

MAX

Yeees

MINTSEV
Hi, Yury Mintsev.

MAX

Hi, Yura.

Mintsev

Max, stay.

MAX
Shelikhovsky breached the gentlemen's agreement. I am **tired** and I'm leaving.

EPISODE 102 INT. RESTAURANT IN NOVOSIBIRSK. EVENING.

MAX
... That's it.

SHELIKHOVSKY
Was it me who fucked her?

MAX
(grabbing his mouth) Relative.

SHELIKHOVSKY
I wanted to help... Well-intentioned road to hell ... Shit overeat.

MAX
And you did. It was right to do so. Buy 3,000 Azot shares at a stock exchange price, 350?

SHELIKHOVSKY
And what do I get from it?

MAX
It's all inside the price.

SHELIKHOVSKY
I bought.

MAX
Delivered. A few shots?

ШЕЛИХОВСКИЙ
A few shots. To not spoiling our relationship.

MAX
And I'll drink to spoil...

CHAPTER 9. MAY 2011. POLITICAL MARRIAGE.

EPISODE 103 NAT. FOOTBALL STADIUM. DAY

At the stadium, during a football match in Kemerovo, Shelikhovsky is sitting with his son and Murashka with a beautiful daughter. (Kemerovo wins Sakhalin. The scoreboard shows 1: 0.

KSYSHA
Russia! Russia! Russia!

SHELIKHOVSKY
Kseniya supports Russia.

MAX
Why are you screaming? Our team wears yellow (Kemerovo).

SHELIKHOVSKY
I wanted to pull you out of depression.

MAX

Goal! During the game ... During the game it was time to score, but not during a penalty ... there was a missed penalty into the gates of Sakhalin during the game)

PART OF THE GAME. MAX'S AND SHELIKHOVSKY'S FACES. MAX LOOKING AT HIS DAUGHTER.

CHAPTER 10. JUNE 2013. DEBRIEFING.

EPISODE 104 INT. BCS OFFICE. DAY.

SHELIKHOVSKY

(Looking up from the table at Max who has just entered the room) I have no money. I sit here ... I sign the papers. (Signs) I am in charge of some household issues now..

Pause.

MAX

Maybe I'll give you money!? FIVE million rubles (shows five fingers)

Pause.

SHELIKHOVSKY

Five already... It used to be three. Shall I leave? It's impossible to work with the director... Moscow is complaining. (he stands up and pretends to be leaving). How shall I leave? A am beneficiary.

MAX

Sit... I am not going to swap places.

SHELIKHOVSKY

An office in London was opened ... I bought an office in Kemerovo ... Everything has changed now. And no one gives a fuck about it.

MAX

I left. I am not interested in what happens at your place.

Murashka takes a pen drive out of his pocket.

MAX

Script. I will sell myself to the Americans... Hollywood is stuck, they've got no ideas. And even if you change the names, everyone will understand who the characters are.
But changing the names ... (with a puzzled grimace)

SHELIKHOVSKY

(red, changes his place for the one in front) I kept waiting. When you will tell me this, at the end. A movie. About fucking? What are you doing?! And why now?

MAX

Rubout. BCS turned 18 years old. Money fuckwad and no bickering. That's how we had to start! Russian style! It's only me who can ride like this.

SHELIKHOVSKY
There is still bickering, but less. All have got out. Raiding ... I will talk to the lawyers ... You rubbed everybody out. And without a single bullet.

MAX

Fine. My father told me: reach the age of 70 and do whatever you want. And I told myself - reach 40. Father ... was a man of unbending will.

SHELIKHOVSKY
You are cooler than your father. Of course, this is a battle between MATRIARCHY and PATRIARCHY.

MAX
Or a battle between good and evil. You have changed a lot. You look great.

SHELIKHOVSKY
I became calm. You lobotomized me - like in "One Flew Over the Cuckoo's Nest", without tools...

MAX
If Bykov took my place in the office and started to buy shares and then. Go and fuck me (well, go and fuck him...) I would have fucked him so much! And I remained the same as I used to be. I wish somebody fucked me.

SHELIKHOVSKY
You said it yourself - fuck... Now that I think about it, I cannot understand - what did I do wrong?

MAX

It was all a right thing to do.

SHELIKHOVSKY

(shakes his head) I should have fucked her. And I sold it for enormous amount of money, at that time.
And I always forget about her sister.
How it all happened, I can not understand so far... A Beautiful Mind. (looking up at Max).

MAX (CHANGING THE TOPIC)

What's next? They will stop printing money and we'll face collapse. Or hyperinflation and war. Buy gold bullions ......

SHELIKHOVSKY

And the war ... That's a reality - there will be a war ... I agree. This is a forecast. And here we are - the schemers. How is your wife? I heard that she left. Is she seeing someone?

MAX

She has no one. During a Lehman case, with a laugh, I did not give her a divorce. Everything can change. I earned. Not lost ...

SHELIKHOVSKY

And I was waiting for you to crawl asking for help finally ... At Lehman case you started drinking. Indeed, money fuckwad, nobody dumped anyone, nobody killed anyone, what happened?

MAX

Tragic accident. Sister. Irina was the first person whom I beat first.

SHELIKHOVSKY
How's your daughter?

MAX
Oh, great. An excellent pupil. I recently bought an apartment for them. Now for you, girl ...
(smiling))

SHELIKHOVSKY
The Americans say the same. Nail their babes.

MAX
Who is their? Do you know where you got busted?

SHELIKHOVSKY
(he shudders) **Girl for a separate sum of money** ... You need to open a brothel. Of course - this is mean ... What?

MAX
Mean is not to nail babes, it is to bicker without a reason. You got busted on AGAIN and AGAIN... trying to fuck me. And I didn't fuck you.

SHELIKHOVSKY
And now you fucked me up. That is, you still did not fuck me? Infinity ... You never fucked anyone, it's impossible to blame you for anything.

MAX
I am a doctor. The script is a bitter medicine. Who fucked whom - is this the main question of being? And what did you get, what did you achieve? Great Depression! Depression among youngsters is rolling over.

SHELIKHOVSKY

I am a nurse. I agree that is a forecast. That's who I am. Send me the script.

MAX

You shouldn't have spoilt the relationship… This is the only way to do!!!

EPISODE 105 INT CAFE DAY.

A WOMAN WHO KEPT SILENT

Max and Natalya are sitting at a half-empty cafe table.

NATALYA

We'll settle for 30% of the apartment ... Repair: my 700 thousand, and nerves, and my back that's put out, I am already tortured by curing.

MAX

Why were you silent? It's Feminism that brings this up. All comes out of frustrated nerves! I wonder if you're going to Hollywood with me. Yes, and do you have a man? And what kind of a man is hiding?

NATALYA

(irritatedly) I don't have anyone!

MAX

Then the question will be: why are you afraid of me? What are you hiding? The script is not finished without you. I can give a divorce. And you can come back in any case. You fell for fear. No excuse for lying.

Natalya keeps silent.

(continues)

The terms of the divorce will be the following.
1st: The daughter will be traumatized and there will be a HARD COMPETITIVE FIGHT for her.
2nd: Complete denial of financial assistance.
3rd: 30% of the apartment goes to Ksenya.
Or - you will be my wife to the grave.
You pull someone FROM MUD, and then you are thrown away.

NATALYA

You didn't pull me out of mud !!! You trampled me into it! Marrying you I loved you and you knew it. And you always wiped your feet on me! When you had problems with your father - I worried and felt sympathy. All what you returned to me was only pain and tears! nothing else!!!

MAX

I did not love you. And did not know. For a reason. And who pulled? Yourself. This is what the method is about.

NATALYA

Yes, I try to pull myself out. I don't love anybody.

MAX

Life without love is nothing. Don't you love your daughter?

NATALYA

I love her. We are divorced. You have no rights to her.

MAX
I will traumatize my daughter.
Hate is better than indifference.
Well-intentioned road to hell ...
You have 30 minutes - and I call
her. If I give a divorce, there
will be no way back..

NATALYA
No, Maxim, I don't need divorce.
My dear and beloved one.

MAX
Good. That's who I am.

EPISODE 106 NAT. STREETS OF THE CITY. DAY.

Max is walking along the sun-lit streets of Kemerovo,

Writing a text to Shelikhovsky.

Shall we make up?

There comes an immediate response.

For sure!

He writes another text.

Peace.

CHAPTER 11. FEBRUARY 2017.DEADLINE.

EPISODE 107 INT. FINANCIAL ADVISER OFFICE. DAY.
The end of February 2017. Chronicle: footage of wars in Ukraine and Syria. Terrorist attacks. Disorder.
Stock charts, oil prices and currency quotes.

Max and a financial adviser are sitting at the table in the office of the BCS branch.

The woman turns a T-shirt in her hands, looking at it curiously.

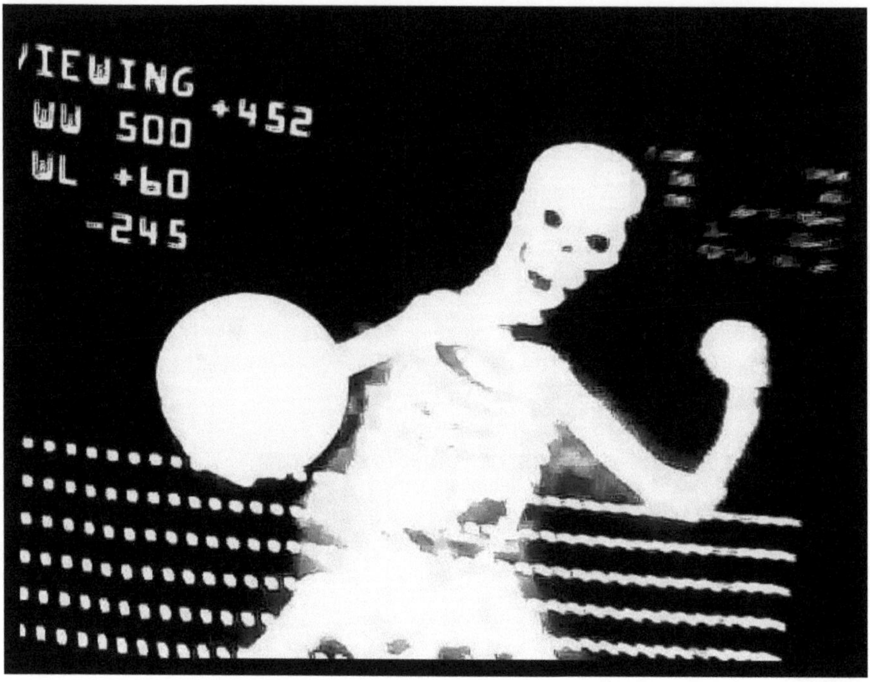

FINANCIAL ADVISER
Send it to the Director General?... Mikhasenko?

She touches half of the "code" - cardboard.

(continues)
And this?

MAX
Yes. I have the second half. Deadline is on the 1st of April.

FINANCIAL ADVISER
The date is meaningful...

MAX
Everything is meaningful... The speculator (my wife) was sold, the analyst (fuck) was sold, the regulator (myself) is being sold, **the daughter** is not for sale. Kindly mpay for my work. As stipulated.

Max points his finger at the number on the T-shirt. There is $ 5,000,000 on a cardboard attached with clips to a T-shirt, the signature is Murashka. Torn edge (dress code).

FINANCIAL ADVISER
The script is attached. (looks at the script in front of her)

MAX
I advise that you read it once again.

FINANCIAL ADVISER
Will you go to settle it? The director will say that he holds a grudge on him...

MAX
(smirking) **Director did not know...**
I told you everything. If there are questions, I will answer.

EPISODE 108 INT/NAT. DIRECTOR'S OFFICE/IN THE STREETS OF THE CITY

Cut-ins (3-4 seconds - the image goes against the background of the calendar, turning to the end of the deadline):

Scenes in the branch of the BCS - the director calls, looking at Max's T-shirt on the table in front of him. Max is having fun with a girlfriend, sitting at the monitor.
Scenes in the branch of BCS - fin. advisor sends mail with a T-shirt.

EPISODE 109 FINANCIAL ADVISOR'S OFFICE. DAY. AFTER APRIL, 1ST

Max and the financial adviser sit at the table in the office again.

FINANCIAL ADVISER
I asked the director of the branch. He said that the T-shirt is destroyed by BCS security service.

MAX

T-shirt or money!

The financial adviser dials a number.

FINANCIAL ADVISER
(talking to the receiver) He needs either T-shirt, or money...

A VOICE IN THE RECEIVER
(after a short pause)
Tell him I don't know where the T-shirt is.
I offer a new one in return.

FINANCIAL ADVISER
(hangs up and puts the phone on the table)
He doesn't knpw where the T-shirt is.
Offers a new one...

MAX
I need my iconic T-shirt - forecast - mascot, of the year 13th! And in general, after the deadline negotiations are not conducted. That is really, here you have exactly nothing to do with it.

Max gets up and walks out of the office. Stops at the door.

MAC
They have torn my T-shirt... and I **tear a peace treaty and take all my assets out of BCS.**

Titles:
(tiker)

Some information:
Profession (on which all investment houses in the Russian Federation were based): the buyer of shares from the population was doomed to death from the very beginning, as the shares ended.
Murashka worked with BCS since 2003 till 2017.
Vasiliev went broke, he is married and has two children.
Irina, after having got fired and experienced a long-term depression, got married and arranged her life in Novosibirsk.
Julia got married, gave birth to a child.
Vasya has become a successful programmer, and he still has no family.
Shelikhovsky's mother committed suicide.
BCS thrives, 99% of the public has gone or been fired since then.
Svetlana divorced Vitaly. Happy in the new marriage.

Dedicated to my daughter Ksenya ...

Предложение о досудебном урегулировании.

К: Шелиховскому В. А. , Михасенко О. В. (Компания БКС)

От: Мурашка М. В.

Претензии в:

1. Сексуальном домогательстве.
2. Угрозах убийством.
3. Вмешательстве в личную жизнь.
4. Вымогательстве.
5. Оскорблении человеческого достоинства.
6. Кражи интеллектуальной собственности.
7. Невыполнении обязательств.
8. Бесчеловечности.

Основание: произведение «Репутация», по адресу https://vk.com/id163785365 или дополнительно по запросу.

Ущерб: утрата трудоспособности, за исключением специфических видов деятельности.

Требование к возмещению: семь миллионов долларов США.

Подпись (Мурашка Максим Викторович):

P.S. С надеждой на возвращение порядочности.

MIX
Papier aus verantwortungsvollen Quellen
Paper from responsible sources
FSC® C105338

Printed by Books on Demand GmbH, Norderstedt / Germany